IT ENDS WITH ME

BREAKING THE CYCLES THAT KEEP US STUCK

DEBBRA BLOSNICH

Copyright © [2023] by [Debbra Blosnich]

All rights reserved.

No portion of this book may be reproduced in any form without written permission from the publisher or author, except as permitted by U.S. copyright law.

Published by Powerful Books

Contents

Introduction	1
My Inner Child	4
Chapter 1	6
Chapter 2	11
Chapter 3	15
Chapter 4	18
Final Words	21
Acknowedgements	22
Relationship Journal	23
Finances Journal	24
Spirituality Journal	25
Health Journal	26
Mental Health Journal	27
Loving Me Journal	28
Daily Gratitude Journal	29

Introduction

We all have a history that shapes who we become. We may not realize how events impact us until much later. In my case, I was living my life repeating patterns until I could no longer ignore the fact that although I felt in control and generally lived a productive, happy life, I lived as a "partial" self. I had learned to cope so well that even I was unaware of my story and history's impact on me. I chose to wake up to myself and, in doing so, found my voice and a calling to share my account so others could find their voice as well.

I have chosen to write this book to bring awareness to the hidden effects trauma, specifically Childhood Sexual Abuse, has on a person. We are living a life loving others but not ourselves. The impact shame has on a person. People who know your story will value you less or think poorly of you. The realization that we are expected to keep quiet, and we did. We silenced our souls. We did this to protect them, ourselves, and our reputation, or so we thought.

When we were asked to go through this life, loving people who stole our innocence, love the ones who were supposed to love and protect us, but instead, they violated our trust and our bodies. When we complied because they are "our family" and "families protect each other." We were asked to neglect ourselves. We were asked to betray ourselves, and we were asked to put on a false show. This made us feel shame and embarrassment. None of which was ours to bear. We took on the labels ourselves that should have been placed on our abusers. We may not even have been consciously aware of these things. I was not. These labels were so engrained in me that I suffered enough, more than enough, until it became unbearable, and I was awakened to my true self, my actual value. I thought I was doing the best I could. I held my secret, never telling anyone the whole story.

Until we reach this point, we never feel worthy enough of happiness or genuine love. We never feel good enough to raise our standards. We try, but it always seems to come with a lesson. That lesson always seems to be, "You do not deserve better." "You had choices." "You can't blame your life on your past."

However, when you are raised in an environment where your innermost thoughts and feelings contradict your life, you change. You are not your true self. Lies and mixed messages about love and your body shape your whole life. "I love you, but I will violate your body." "I love you, but your well-being is less important than my need to feel power and control." "I love you, but I can't look bad in front of others." And yes, we choose based on a warped sense of self and worthiness. We see others as more deserving, and we hope we will be excellent and worthy to someone. Of course, we fall prey to other hurt people who seek to validate themselves by exerting their power over us. If we can see some value in ourselves, we release some of our shame and guilt. We may be able to lead somewhat of a "normal" life.

In my case, as I know others have. I had handled it well enough. I thought I was doing alright. I never gave up, always had hope, yet I always found myself with the worst partners. They cheated, lied, ignored, or physically harmed me. I felt strong because I always walked away when it reached the point of being too painful. Finally, after the last betrayal by my abuser (my father), by my mother (she could not choose us or the truth), and by my latest intimate partner. I was walking away for the last time and vowed never again. Never again would I devalue myself. Never again would I let someone into my world who didn't earn their place here. I woke up to the truth. I was not healed, and as loving as I was to others, I had not extended that love to myself. Now I know I am learning, I am a fantastic person, and I deserve amazing people in my life.

It ends with me. The cycle of abuse end here, now. I will heal myself. I will go boldly to share my story and end the shame of what was done to me for me and those who need to do the same. These generational curses that plague our families have to complete.

I let it all go. It wasn't my fault. I was a child whose innocence was st en, whose identity was tarnished. I had been brave and strong for far too long.

From now on, I will love myself with the same love I have for others. I know love is supportive. Love cares when you are hurt. Love uplifts and encourages. Love seeks to help you become your best self. Love appreciates who you are. Love accepts your faults but requires you to rise above them when necessary and improve. Love wants you to be safe and happy. Love is a place to be your true self. Love is reciprocal. It cherishes you and celebrates you. Love wants to see the love you give returned to you tenfold. Love sees your pain and wipes away your tears. Love opens its arms and offers a safe place to lay it all down and know you are loved.

Find the love you are so deserving of and give it to yourself!!

I decided to create a book that is also a journal that will hopefully start you on a journey to loving yourself and seeing yourself as the exceptional individual you are.

My Inner Child

Dear Inner Child,

Hello, my beautiful girl. You are so sweet and full of love. I am here for you. I see you. I see you have been hurt.

You were not supposed to have this in your life. You were meant to be cherished and taken care of. I am here for you. You are safe. You can relax now; I've got you. I will hold you as long as you need me to. I will not let anyone harm you. You are free to love and experience life. I know you have been hiding, cautious, afraid of who will hurt you next. You will no longer have to fear others. I have seen the harm done to you and witnessed the effects of your decisions. You thought you had healed and found your way. You were lost while trying to find your way in this world.

We know now. Love is uplifting and brings us joy. Love does not hurt us. Love makes us feel safe and secure. Love is not self-serving. Love will make a way for us to grow and be joyful. You can come out now when you feel threatened. I assure you I have your back. You have nothing to fear. Your shame and your guilt can be released. They were not yours to carry. Everything you did or did not do, you did to protect yourself in the only way a child could.

I did my best to forgive and love and move on. I've since learned that we were not healed and not okay. We were seeking love in the way we knew it. Full of neglect and deceit, and unavailability. We felt comfortable amongst liars and abusers. So when we encountered them at first, they felt good and comfy. Luckily I was able to see them in their truth. It hurt to find us compromised again. But now we are safe. I have finally become aware of the patterns we were following. I can see our truth. We were betrayed by the person and people who were supposed to protect us. So we felt unworthy, and we could not set healthy boundaries. We thought we had to understand others. We confused compassion for self-neglect. We no longer allow harm to come to us. Our body knows before we do. We listen. We no longer wait to see what evil lurks behind the façade. We walk away, wishing them peace.

We hold our heads high and keep moving forward. Our story is not over. Come with me now, and let's create a more beautiful future for us and those we love.

Love,

Me.

Thank You.

Chapter 1

I am six years old. I am giddy and happy, and playful. I live with my mom and dad and have an older sister and a younger sister.

One evening my dad called me to his room. I joyfully go to see what he wants. "Touch me, he - (here)" That's all I can remember about that moment. I return to my room, and my sister asks me something like, "Did he touch you?" I don't know; I think I said "yes."

I only remember snippets of past events like this one. I woke up one evening with him on top of me while I was asleep in the top bunk of a bunk bed. He tried to penetrate me. I said, "Ouch, it hurts." He didn't stab me. I don't think. I don't remember much of what happened over the years; I remember conversations after "it" was done. "This is normal in some places." Later, "I can't get you pregnant; I've been fixed." I didn't even know what he was talking about. I was nine. I was sore the next day.

My mom asked me once when I was nine. "Does your dad do anything to you?" I lied; I said, "No, not really. He sometimes walks in on me when I'm in the shower." There was never another word about it. The abuse continued until I left for college at eighteen. I went two weeks after I graduated high school. I am free. My older sister, younger sister, younger brother, and youngest sister are still there. It makes me worried, but I go.

During the Spring of my first year. My younger sister says she is going to tell the police. Don't tell our older sister. Of course, I told my older sister. We talk, and we share our stories a little bit. The police are called. My dad leaves for a while. I don't know what happened because I was at school safe. My older sister and I attended the same school. We hung out once or twice as we were dealing with this stuff. My younger sister, the one who spoke up, is sick. We want to go home and see her. Everyone says, "Stay there." We don't visit; we don't go home. We stay at school. At some point during my finals week. Some lawyer calls and says, "Do you want to press charges? You're the only one who can, based on time frames." Oh my God!! Uhm... no, I don't. I suddenly realized this abuse started at six until I was eighteen. This was my family, and they were good to me and loved me. Life has been like this for twelve years of my life. It cannot be my fault this family goes to shit.

The semester ends, and I take as long as possible to go home. I spend a long weekend with friends, and finally, I do go home. My friends say they are worried; I am so quiet. I say nothing.

At home, nothing is new. My sister is gone for a little while. She is with friends. Life continues. My mom and dad are acting as though life is normal. We all went to some counseling, horrible!! The counselors cry. Other children who have been abused are there; their stories are terrible. Some want to live with their abusive fathers instead of going with their mom. My head reels. They ask a few simple questions. "Are you promiscuous?" WTF!!! I tell them there was another adult who sexually abused me as well when I was 12. "We're not going to talk about that." Again, WTF!!! Okay, I don't know what this therapy is about, but I take notes. I hear it is not about sex; it's about control. It's not your fault. Okay, fine, but I feel some aspects or other things related to it could be. Like my younger sister being hurt. I had told him never to touch her, only me. "Leave her alone!" I thought he might listen. What did I know? I was twelve at the time.

The point here is nothing happened. Nothing changed. I cannot say exactly what I thought. I know life went on as usual—no more sexual abuse toward me. I didn't talk to my sister about her. Although I guess I figured if she told the police, he wasn't doing anything anymore. Especially after she was gone for a while.

Life goes on. I graduated college and got married, and had two beautiful children. Two boys. Sometimes I feel weird about them around my dad. But he only hurt us girls, so he would never hurt them. But he's impatient at times, and it makes me uneasy.

I got divorced. I met a man who was also divorced and had kids. Okay. He wanted to move in. He's horrible, mean, controlling, and lazy. I suddenly realize I'm pregnant. I let him stay. I want to look like a good person. The next three years are hell. He's verbally, mentally, and physically abusive, but only occasionally. I told him that he needed to leave. It's not easy; the courts won't hear me. Nobody sees the truth. I get most of the custody while he gets some weekends. After many months I got a PFA. (Protection From Abuse order.) He violates it. Goes away for a month. He violates it. He is going away for two months. He violates again. Nobody will arrest him. I worry for my son but believe he will always be okay.

Three years later, his dad tried to use my story against me. He accuses me of being sexually abusive toward our son. He blames my son of being a sexual predator at age six. The courts don't see anything, and we continue shared custody.

I'm still going on with life as "I'm normal." I work as a teacher; I'm raising my three boys. I go back to school for a better position. I keep going. Ten years go by.

Mother's Day. I've stopped by to say hello to my mom. My sister stops by with her family. She has been keeping her distance for a few months, not feeling right about our dad. They say hello, and my mom asks for some help in the yard. "Your dad can't do it; he's not feeling well." They help. Later that night, my niece, thirteen, tells her mom something weird happened.

When I hear this I want to kill him. "Are you for real? All this time. I always yelled at you and told you how you hurt me. Us. How can you do this?!! How could we all be so stupid!!"

It ends now. He is dead to us: me and my sister. My mom is told. She says, "I'm sorry." She stays again. We ask her to get out. Leave him. She can't. This goes on for a year. We see our mom. She comes to events alone. She still mentions him to us. We tell her we don't care. Please don't talk to us about him. She can't stop. This is our mom. The woman who attends mass daily. Visits the sick.

Helps anyone in need. She has a big heart. She loves God. How come she can't do this for us? How can she stay? How come she never left before?

The following Easter. She accuses my sister of sexually assaulting her son. That is it for me; I'm out. I'm raging inside. How could you? What!!? This woman, your daughter, is over here protecting her children from your husband, a monster, and you're going to accuse her!!! I cannot. I tell my mom to stay away. She stops by unannounced, and I try to talk to her. What were you thinking? How could you? No answer will do. There is no answer she can give that makes me understand. I yell at her. I am sad that I yelled at her. I'm dying because this woman was my friend. I cared for her and included her in everything. I made sure she enjoyed life—my family. Oh I am so upset. I call a counselor; he says cut that festering mess out of your life. I do.

My mom gets sick. She's in and out of the hospital. I go to see her. I see him. This could be it. My sisters and I talk about how this is so hard. What have these two done to all of us? It lasts three months. To the hospital, rehab, and back to the hospital. Who's going to do this? Who's going to do that? Guess what? Not me. I lost my mom three months ago. I cried then. I mourned the loss of what I thought I had, what I wished I'd had. A loving mother who cared. The truth hurts. What was real? What is real? Did she love us at all? Was she so consumed in "looking" right in the eyes of others that she let us be subjected to all of this?

The battle cry was always. "Don't tell anyone. They will use it against you." It's working against me now!!! It always has. This silence. This keeps our story quiet—this facade of love. Damn, I mean, I loved you with all my heart. I forgave you and him as much as humanly possible. I let you in my life. I allow you to be a part of my family, be grandparents. Now, that's all gone, and as I realize now. It should never have happened. You two were self-centered, horrible people.

I had met another guy. I was skeptical but he seemed nice, he lived out of town. But we needed a break from a man in our house. Nine years went by. He has always been friendly, loving, and supportive. He knows a little of my story. He knows about the horrible past relationship I had. He says that wasn't right and I am safe with him. He could be distant sometimes, but plans and such were discussed. I start to feel something... I have to check his phone. Bam! World shattered again. I am a pawn in his sick game. He never cared, and his game is meeting as many women as possible, creating false relationships with them, and leading them on to fill his insatiable need for validation. I'm dumbstruck.

This relationship ends. I try as much as possible not to talk to my dad. Only at the hospital when I visit my mom. Those are hard days. She says crazy stuff. He acts like he doesn't know why I'm distant. My mom passed away. I say sweet relief to her and us. We cannot keep this up very long. Too much damage, too much betrayal. I know they were hurt children who grew up rough but come on. You knew better. He sought out information about everything. Why didn't he take the time to learn about why he is the way he is? She loved God so much. She forgot to have faith and walked away to help her children.

Now, we are healing. I started healing the day I walked away from my mom. After my counselor told me to cut them out. I did in my heart. I cried a lot. There was so much loss. So much betrayal. There is also healing and, most importantly ME. I am here. I am love. It ends with me (and my strong-ass sisters). It ends here. It ends now.

That was my story up until now. The rest of the story remains to be seen. I can tell you it will be glorious. I have found my voice. I am here for me and for anyone who needs me. How did I get here, you ask??? Read on.

Chapter 2

I lived my life in survival mode. Now, I didn't realize this until I was much older. Well, I guess until about a year ago. So I'm now fifty-three years old. For fifty-three years, I hid, smiled, and did what I was supposed to do.

I also want you to know. I didn't feel like I was being "fake" or "false." I thought I was being genuine, sincere, compassionate, and empathetic. I generally felt happy and content. Looking back, I was hiding from the world. I didn't want anyone to "know" me. "What would they think?" They would know my shame, my dirty secret. Whenever I came close to sharing or did share, it only caused more pain. Nobody seemed to care anyway. "Everyone has their story/pains in life." I would think, "But everyone else can say their pain; nobody will understand this." (my story). "This is the *thing* nobody talks about." "I wasn't raped or molested by a stranger; I was raped and molested by my dad." And even when authorities knew, the church knew... nothing happened. So with all of that, I thought. You get angry, yell at them, forgive, and move on. You live.

What I didn't know was what I do now. Growing up like this wires you a certain way. People who feel safe with you are dangerous. They feel at home; they feel comfortable; you know this feeling. They think this way because they like the people they grew up with. They are friendly (to a point), but they are needy, act needy, and hurt. They use their "weakness" to pull you in. "What kind of person wouldn't understand that someone who's been hurt wouldn't have some scars, some issues?"

Only looking back now do I realize. I'm the kind of person who has been severely betrayed, abused, neglected, and ignored, and I do not bring pain to those who love me. I love people. I care. I want everyone to feel safe, loved, and appreciated. I want you to love yourself!!

So the pattern runs. I meet someone; We get along. They are friendly, fun. They are attentive; they tell me I'm beautiful, intelligent, and kind. I may or may not tell them a tiny sliver of my story. "I was traumatized as a child." Oh, well, okay. I'm sorry. I would never hurt you. They don't run, though. I feel happy and relieved. I am worthy of them. Then as things go on, I realize a few things. They are distant and unavailable (literally or mentally and emotionally) for deep connection. They cheat, they lie, they hide who they are. They gaslight me into believing I am the problem here. So I try to love, give, and be more worthy of them. They aren't safe for me. I think, "They have been hurt.", "They're doing the best they can." "Deep down, they love me." "They did that nice thing the other day, week, month." They tell me I'm beautiful, intelligent, and kind. They didn't leave me. "But then why is he acting like ...." I think it, I see it, I feel it. It must be me; I'm sensitive because of my past.

The absolute truth is they don't care; they are incapable. They were hurt, but they never healed themselves. They are out hurting others. In my experience, they know they are w and are hurting you and do it. It is who they are.

So, as I started "waking up" and seeing the truth. I learned a few things about growing up and living with the secret of incest:

- You don't respect yourself

- You're not very good at setting healthy boundaries

- Deep down, you do not value yourself

- You live feeling shame

- You live feeling guilt

- You live feeling dirty and used

- You feel comfortable around people who come off as calm, relaxed rule-breakers.

- You hide so no one will see you because if they knew the truth, they wouldn't understand

- Your body senses the "bad" in people

- BUT....

- You will ignore your body and blame it on your past

- You will lie to yourself, "Everyone deserves love,"; he "It's not that bad."

I love genuinely because I do not want anyone to experience what I have. I want everyone to know that they are loved; they are loveable and worthy, and beautiful. That kind of stings because God loves all of his children. God does not want us to suffer, though, and he does not want us to stay where we are harmed.

The difference between before I woke up and now. I learned some fantastic things:

- I deserved better

- I am worthy of love. The kind of love that raises you up. The type of love that lets you express all of your emotions. The kind of love that enables you to know you are safe and valuable and you are worth protecting.

- I learned my abuse was not me

- I can release my shame. It was never mine to carry.

- I am beautiful

- I am caring

- I am a loving soul

- I am deserving of respect and love, and care

I also learned a little girl was hiding, afraid, inside of me. She is me—the girl I rescued. And nobody could find her and help her, except for me. She is here now. She is safe. I will protect her. Now, we go together. We grow together. Our lesson has been learned.

I am beautiful. My soul is love. I know how to love, and now I love ME. I respect ME. I cherish ME. I honor ME. I love my silly ways, and I love my serious side. I treat everyone with love and respect. But now I learned to love myself first. I learned to trust my gut. If it feels "Wrong," I let it be. I walk away from the "bad." I no longer question myself. I do not need to know what it is; I do not wait to see what kind of "bad" is coming. I trust. Trust ME. I know what love is. It's what I give to myself. It's that thing I always saw in others as a reflection of myself. I was unable to see them. I do now.

There is no space for anything but love now.

Chapter 3

First, I sought out professional help. I needed someone familiar with this type of trauma to help me process what was happening now. They let me let go. Guilt Free.

I read about healing:
- From Narcissists (they can only think of themselves)

- From Trauma bonds (we get so entangled it is hard to let go - but you were in love with the idea of who they were, not them)

- Inner Child Work - you have to go and find you - the lost you - the helpless you and rescue them - protect them

- I watched daily - TikTok videos about all of the parts of me that hurt
    - Abused as a child/ as an adult
    - Survival mode - how it wrecks you physically and mentally
    - Self-love - be your own best friend - she would love you exactly as you indeed are

Personal Development:
- Let go of that old story - it's history, and your future is waiting

- Use the past to rise and fuel your passion

- Identify your circle of influence - you cannot control everything or anyone - But you can control yourself, your thoughts, and actions - you can be a light to others.

- I am worthy

- I am powerful

- I have a purpose / I have purpose

- Somebody needs me

- Forgiveness - forgiveness does not mean you forget, justify or lessen your story

- Forgiveness means: I no longer allow the past to control me. I am in control. I am free to let go knowing I am safe now. I will choose better now.

- I do not need to live in fear

- I do not need to live in shame or guilt or shadows

- I will let my light shine and shine brightly as it was always meant to

My light is meant to shine as a beacon. Lighting the way for others out of the dark.

Now I talk to myself as if I'm talking to my best friend. (And I am - for in the end - nobody knows me better than me). I give myself all the loving support I would a best friend. I give her the following:

- Love

- Respect

- A safe space

- Grace

- Encouragement

- Forgiveness

- Space for ALL of her - I let her feel ALL her feelings. I remind her how far she has already come and has yet to go.

Chapter 4

My story isn't over yet, and neither is yours. We are not promised tomorrow. So as long as my journey continues, I (you) must discover who I (you) really are. And I will work daily on becoming the best me I can be. And I will remind myself daily.

I am:
Love
Beautiful
Kind
Courageous
Unstoppable
Fierce
Gentle
Full of joy
Full of hope
Energetic
Compassionate
Honorable
Trustworthy
An advocate
Smart
I am.

I know who I am and who I want to become. I am constantly growing and learning and becoming more ME. I am human, so I fall but get up, and the world needs me. It requires me to be my best. I need to show the world that love is real. There is always hope as long as we keep going.

I keep journals now.

- Gratitude Journal: to remind me there is always something to be grateful for

- Loving Me Journal:
    - What am I doing to honor myself
    - What am I doing to care for myself
    - What/ Who do I need to say no to?
    - What/ Who do I need to say yes to?

- Life Journal:
    - Where am I emotionally? Is it good or not so good? What am I needing? What can I give to change that?
    - Where am I in my health? Am I treating my body with respect and love? I need to have my health to live my purpose!!
    - Where am I in my relationships? Am I being me? Am I giving and receiving love?
    - Where am I with my finances? Am I being responsible and creating a life of happiness and joy with what I have? Could I be doing more/making more/ giving more?
    - Where am I spiritually? Do I feel connected to the Universe? God? Something bigger than me?

If I find I am missing the mark in an area. It is time to evaluate:
- What is one thing I can do today, this week, and this month to move toward where I want to be?

- Who do I need to help me get there? Accountability partner, a friend, a coach?

- What do I need to do for myself to make it happen?

- Is this for me or others?

I hope this book has brought you to a place where you see you are not alone. You are worthy of all the love in the world. First, you must love yourself. There is hope.

Final Words

You can always start again. You can take all of your life's experiences and choose to choose differently. Choosing to write this book was a huge decision. I did not take it lightly. We are all born full of light and love; the world changes that. The world can also be a place of joy, light, and peace. We must choose who we let in and surround ourselves with.

Learn to love yourself. You are unique and worthy; all you need to do is accept that simple truth. You have nothing to prove to anyone. You were born you perfectly. Search for yourself and choose to be the best you.

ACKNOWEDGEMENTS

Thank you to the ones who loved me even when I wasn't loving myself. Thank you to my sisters for always being loving and supportive badasses all in your own right. They say you are blessed if you have one true friend. I am lucky enough to have 4. My three amazing sisters and one amazing brother.

Thank you to my children who showed me that being perfect isn't the goal. Being a loving, safe space that lets you be you is. I love you with all of me. You are the greatest joys I have ever had the pleasure of experiencing.

Thank you to Perry Power for being so courageous in Breaking Your Silence. Thank you for starting this amazing group and inviting me into it. The work you are doing is priceless and long overdue. The world will be a better place because you opened your ears and heart to others. I love you.

Thank you to Emma for polishing my story and supporting my voice in the most loving way. You are a beautiful soul.

Thank you to the other members of this brave group, the Powerful Books Community. We didn't choose the things done to us, but we are choosing now to take our trauma and be a beacon of hope and change. You are powerful warriors of courage and love and change. You offered a place to be real and loved me. I love you all as well.

Relationships

Where am I in my relationships? Am I being me?

Am I giving and Receiving love?

Am I loving myself?

What is one thing I can do this week to engage more in meaningful ways with myself/ my family/ friends?

"I love myself more so I can love others and they can love me."

Finances

Am I being responsible with my gifts ?

_____
_____
_____

Am I creating a life of joy and happiness with what I have?

_____
_____
_____

Could I be doing more/ Creating more / giving more?

_____
_____
_____

What is one step I can take to take money out of the equation and enjoy life more fully?

_____
_____
_____

"My value is not in my bank account."

Spirituality

Do I feel connected to the Universe? God? Something bigger than me?

_____
_____
_____

Am I expecting the Universe to work in my favor?

_____
_____
_____

Am I asking for guidance and seeking with an open hopeful heart?

_____
_____
_____

Did I take time this day/ week to sit and be still with the universe?

_____
_____
_____

"I belong to the Universe."

Health

How is my health overall?
___
___
___

Am I treating my body with respect and love?
___
___
___

What can I do to increase my health today?
___
___
___

I need my health to live my best life!!
___
___
___

"I treat my body with respect."

Mental Health Journal

Where am I emotionally?
_____
_____
_____

Have I been in a good state or poor state?
_____
_____
_____

What am I needing?
_____
_____
_____

What can I give to change that?
_____
_____
_____

"I do what brings me peace."

Loving Me

What am I doing to honor myself?

_____
_____
_____

What am I doing to care for myself?

_____
_____
_____

What/ Who do I need to say no to?

_____
_____
_____

What / Who do I need to say Yes to?

_____
_____
_____

"I love me as I am"

Daily Gratitude

3 things I'm grateful for today are...

_____
_____
_____

The best part of today was...

_____
_____

What can I learn from today's experiences?

_____
_____
_____

Tomorrow I'm looking forward to...

_____
_____
_____

"I am Grateful for Today"

Made in the USA
Middletown, DE
07 June 2025

76692240R00021